Benedict's Daughter

Benedict's Daughter

Poems

PHILIP C. KOLIN

RESOURCE *Publications* · Eugene, Oregon

BENEDICT'S DAUGHTER
Poems

Resource Publications
An Imprint of Wipf and Stock Publishers
199 W. 8th Ave., Suite 3
Eugene, OR 97401

www.wipfandstock.com

PAPERBACK ISBN: 978-1-5326-1147-6
HARDCOVER ISBN: 978-1-5326-1149-0
EBOOK ISBN: 978-1-5326-1148-3

Manufactured in the U.S.A.   JANUARY 6, 2017

for Margie and Al

I decided after investigating everything carefully from the very first to write an orderly account for you, Theophilus, so that you may know the truth concerning the things about which you have been instructed.

LUKE 1:3

He should know that whoever undertakes the government of souls must prepare himself to account for them.

ST. BENEDICT, *HOLY RULE*

What we love we shall grow to resemble.

ST. BERNARD OF CLAIRVAUX

Humanity, take a good look at yourself. To one side you've got heaven and earth, and all creation. You're a world—everything is hidden in you.

ST. HILDEGARD OF BINGEN

Contents

Acknowledgments

MY THANKS GO TO the following journals where some of these poems originally appeared:

"A Hospice Crucifixion"	*ARTS*
"A Manual for Oblates"	*St. Austin Review*
"A Nurse Called Joseph"	*Blood and Thunder*
"The Bridegroom Comes"	*Christian Century*
"The Garden"	*Third Wednesday*
"God's Favorite Language"	*Catholic Lane*
"Holy Communion Is"	*Emmanuel*
"Midge"	*Penwood Review*
"In the Month of Blue Moons"	*Third Wednesday*
"Mr. Al Goes Fishing"	*Blood and Thunder*
"Midge"	*Third Wednesday*

Introduction

THESE POEMS TELL THE story of a remarkable woman of faith, a spiritual director for over 50 years who lived her life according to St. Benedict's *Holy Rule*. Interspersed with poems about her and her family are those that focus directly on Benedictine spiritual traditions, liturgies, saints, and abbeys.

PART 1

Prologue: The Liturgy of the Hours

Lauds

Day Opens

The book of day opens with
the papery feel of dew on azure;
sun shafts sign the distant hilltops
overlooking the abbey
with heaven's new covenant.

It's time to shake off
the mortality of sleep;
the tomb of night is cracked, step out

and feel the infinity of light.
Dawn has resurrected the world
from the denial of darkness.

The air is inscribed with Gospels
calling us to be a part of forever:
the *Angelus* and Mass bells,
the canticles of rivers and oceans,
and the blessings of soft-voiced breezes—
all ring souls with delight.

God fills daybreak with himself.

Terce

St. Peter on the Eternity of Three

Everything I learned about eternity unfolded
in threes. Mary told me about the Magi
and about losing him in the temple

then finding him three days later.
James, John, but I saw her glorified son
transfigured on that holy mountain top.

Coming down, we wiped the dazzle
from our eyes; and for three years
it spread like lilies across the fields.

Then came Gethsemane
and the blood tears he shed
turning stones opalescent red.

That night the high priest's courtyard
felt as cold as my tongue; I denied him
the three times the cock crowed.

I froze at the third hour
when unctuous Pilate
sentenced him to die.

I could not watch those three crosses
standing stark on that hill
or bear to see the temple veil

ripping apart. The darkness
that followed his death
stole three hours' light from the sky.

The third day the women,
Salome, Joanna, Magdela,
ran back from the tomb with earth-

shaking news that he had risen,
the stone rolled away,
and his burial linens lay limp
on the floor.

On Pentecost at the third hour
the Holy Spirit descended
enflaming our tongues

to speak each other's language.
Noised about the city, his promise
fulfilled this hour of sacred prayer.

Sext

The Hour Christ Died

Midday, the sext hour, mealtime
for all the empty eyes waiting
in the long soup lines at St. Meinrad's.

They are Christ suffering—
the homeless, the betrayed, and
the abandoned; children with distended stomachs
wounded by hunger and thirst;
seniors crucified on a fixed income.

They have not read Benedict's *Rule*
on providing hospitality
or giving guests a pound weight of bread,
and pilgrims a hemina of wine.

But they know the black monks
will fill them with all good things:
red jello bouncing like a pounding heart;
meatloaf in thick brown gravy;
mashed potatoes puffy as cumulus clouds in April.

The sun is at its fullest
as they leave; the hour Christ died.
But as they walk out, one
by one, the monks bless each
with a hyssop branch,
dipped in holy water.

Vespers

The Delta Between Sunset and Dark

At this holy hour, the Delta hinges
between the splendor of sunset
and the covetous reach of dark.

Cotton fields dress in Easter white—
brides processing down aisles,
ready to light their lamps, waiting
for the groom.

A cream-draped lotus offers
enticement to the evening air,
a bouquet of incense.

A young girl tells her cousin
about the infinite joy
she carries in her rounding womb.

Lilies drift across the flat, long land
into their silhouettes.

At nightfall the soft
side of sorrow seeps in—
a mother stands alone
beside the body of her lynched son
keening, the melody of grief

picked up by the moanful refrain
of the blues from the clapboard church
across the road.

Through the stained glass windows
the candles look like sunsets.

Compline

The Day is Done

The convent has silenced the sky—
no bell clangs or calls
in this dark season; the day is done;
neither bunting nor jay takes wing;
night masks the earth's green splendor
in mists and mazes.

Before the dim chapel lamp
the sisters beg for light to keep watch over
their thoughts and dreams,
and entreat angels to make rounds
evicting sin-sated whisperers
and phantoms in harlequin disguise.

In their cells, each sister undresses
her conscience, yet again
asking forgiveness for slipping
into vanity or being shackled in shame,
thieves of the day's glory,

and then wills her soul to God
in scapular Latin, cloistered in her bed
(*in manus tuas*), just before she reaches

the shelter of feathers and wings.

PART 2

The Journey

In This Place of Stability

Vow to be part of this holy place
so it can be part of you.

Settle like a tree rooted in a flowering stream
so the years will not wither you.

Be like a harvest of grain and grapes
transformed into Christ's body and blood.

Steadfast yourself like a knoll overlooking the horizon
where angels mix with summer fireflies.

Be at peace here with all creatures
that burrow, swim, roam, or soar.

We are all flesh of flesh until
the bridegroom comes clothed in clouds.

Continue to search for God on these grounds
and let him find you at the crossroads

traveling east to speak with him
as Adam did before Eden was padlocked.

Awake with the dawn to inhale dappled sunlight
and let the hours wash over and anoint you.

Listen for the sound of God's laughter,
but shade your eyes before his jasper tears.

He made this abbey his home for you,
your Nazareth, your Jerusalem.

Grow in holiness in this place
until one day, one night,

your roots become wings.

The Gulls' Oratory

Your body is too frail;
more bones than flesh really.
We are not sure it is strong
enough to keep your soul alive
for a vocation.

The prioress's words
ended her novitiate.
She had to take off
the white veil and Benedictine scapular
and leave the convent.

So many gulls ribboned
Mobile Bay the day she came home,
more than 150 swooping
in their dirty white and molting grey coats.
It was hard to hear God's voice
with all their squawking.

The chapel and her convent cell had provided
a silent, stable place to nurture her soul.
Now the world demanded
tribute for her return. The gulls

never stopped their flapping gossip,
shiftless scavengers leisurely
skimming the bay for the abundance of fish,
always waiting for them. Tourists with handfuls
of bread and washed grapes shout to them.

Why couldn't her road to the kingdom
have been easy like the gulls'. Her vocation
was interrupted so early.
She sowed so many beads on her rosary
and toiled hard to reap God's treasure

buried within. But taking up her life
in the world again, the oratory of the gulls
followed her to Mass, her office, home,
even while praying to St. Scholastica.

She heard parables in their cries:
They have neither storehouses nor barns
yet God feeds them. All this will be given
unto you as well.

She returned often to the bay
to pray with the gulls.

Father Luke, O.S.B.

He taught her to open God's outdoor lectionary
and read the messages written there—

to see the sky as his canvas,
each rainbow a stroke of quiet color;

to look for the faces of the Apostles
in the autumn clouds hanging

close enough to touch,
silvery rosary beads

to meditate on the silence of frost;
and study the longing of trees

to divest themselves of earth's venery
for a new season of austere wonder.

He took her to the sea in winter
to hear terns crying along the shore

answering the muffled waves,
endless dirges of human suffering.

He gave her a test for the soul:
bottle the wind—save it like chrism

from visits by the Holy Spirit,
anointing the air with whirling tongues,

prophesizing the purgation of loss
and the redemption of time.

He asked her to watch snow dislocating
surfaces, transforming furrowed fields

into glazed winding sheets,
roots and seeds below

hoping for a new birth.
She strived to be a small light

for others on their journey
from self to salvation.

The Bridegroom Comes

He fell in love with her jade eyes
searching for him on the river bank

a few miles above Mobile
at her father's fishing camp.

He spoke to her through
Gulf breezes and gray-dawn gulls

and lavished prophecies on her
the way tides speak of the deep.

Anointing her words, he poured
ancient Seraphic chants and

refrains, without rhyme, into her
voice as joyful as timbrels at betrothals.

Next to her curl-edged Bible
she kept her cigarettes, lit lamps

waiting in the moonless, salty night
ready when he called her back

across the river raptured with stars,
their flasks overflowing with oil.

Lenten Wooing

She gave him up
for Lent as quickly

as candy, Bing Crosby,
the movies, or that extra

cigarette after dinner.
He would have

to do penance and wait
to see if the Holy Spirit brought

her back into his life. Forty days of no
dates, touches, sweet words, smiles,

only stolen looks. They were employed
at the same plant in Mobile.

Her desk sat behind a glass partition
he had to pass on the way to his job;

his eyes worked like a nervous glass cutter
whenever he went down that hallway.

But her devotion to denial
and self-discipline carried

over from her convent days
trained her eyes to see right through

him as he walked by; the Spirit would
show her if he was the right one.

When Easter dawned and
the Paschal light shown in him

she knew that some day
they would make love

like angels in the glass-spun air
without sweat or sighs.

Marriage Vows

They stood before
the priest vested in white

hearts ready for vows,
silent and solemn

like a candle.

Mr. Al's Jubilee

Mr. Al grew up in the 1930s
on Mobile's eastern shore;
his mother swept dirt rugs and washed clothes
in the bay; his father worked there, too,
measuring success by the calluses
notched in his hands and
the meals his children
missed. Too often a dinner
plate was as empty
as a rock-snagged net.
He wrote hunger pleas to God
in his mother's tired Bible—
Need food, please help, please;
send angels with bulging flounder.

But his spelling was off
so many times he wondered if
God ever got his messages.
The only time his belly and his soul
felt full came when a Jubilee
fed the beach with more
than 140 species of fish, crabs, and oysters
scrambling on the shore,
ready to be gathered in old croker sacks
and taken home. Memories of Jubilees past
nourished him for decades, long after
he left Mobile. He mounted some of the shells

he saved in the shape of a cross
and hung it in the hallway just outside
their bedroom. God blessed him
and his bride with a rich harvest
of children whom they fed on rosaries
that looked like bobbing fishing lines.

The Child Within

for Andreas

She navigated two souls
in this great sea—

hers and mine.
I am on a voyage

from eternity
through wombed time

to a world of refugees
and falls. I know neither

yet we share paradoxes—
she is my cloister;

I am her psalmody—singing wildly about
the universe inside me.

But paradise has not stopped
speaking to me.

My language still tastes
like angel tongues

and sounds like stringed wonders.
Sometimes she hymns along

the way a translation
comes so close to the original.

She reads saints' lives
to me at mealtime—

Scholastica visiting her brother
just before he ascended

to where my soul was born
and where God's name is everywhere.

At night she and I
listen to each other's hearts

beating like wings
or waves on the shore.

Heaven's metronome,
earth's clocks.

Midge

She was small, hardly
4 feet, 11 inches;
her lumbering brothers
teased her, calling her Midge,
for midget.

Seated, her husband
was as tall as she was high;
but when he hugged her,
she became a valley full of cedars.

Curled up in her Bible
she birthed prayers for those who sought her
after Mass or at the school where she taught.
Souls rang her doorbell; called her name
in the small hours of their mourning.

She was a sleepless angel
counting beads on her rosary
the way an astronomer measures stars.

A hermit ate more lavishly; she fasted
even during green harvest months
to feed famished souls
a taste of how endless heaven could be.

She Taught Her Classes Proverbs

She taught her classes proverbs
helping students to grow holy

from the inside out—
first they had to befriend

the skeletons they wore
under their flesh.

God's blueprint calls for
nature to cooperate with grace.

Students then had to remove
the barbed wire strung across

their tongues; pernicious words
only smothered flowers.

Be wary of pretense, too;
it's a corrosive color

beggaring integrity
and boring holes in your armor.

Travel inside your minds,
she taught, into that vast

and diverse bounty
of lyrics and logarithms

where mercies are multiplied
and full moons dance.

Love is a high-plains country
where you can learn a new language.

Breathe air scented with hyacinths
so your voice sounds like a garden.

Look for stars like mirrors
that remember your face.

Smoke can shelter mysteries
as well as fire.

Both are necessary to see
the burning bush God lights for you.

Finally, search for the hidden
part of yourself

always in others' hearts,
unexpected sanctuaries.

God's Favorite Language

After compline, Brother Leo
started his wordless pilgrimage
around St. Bernard's
canopied with stars that sang their light.

He prayed in less heard places,
and he spoke more to God
and less to men. In silence
he abstained from self.

It became his passport
into the kingdom to come.
His prayers were invisible
like the God whom he served

but who spoke to him
in the Creator's favorite language
to share mysteries and prophecies,
and listen to the conscience of the monks.

The best conversations with God
never burst forth from rippling lips
but from sealed mouths
and open souls.

Brother Leo longed to go to the desert
where the air still held silent prayers
said centuries ago by holy men
with fasting beards.

The Spiritual Son

He showed up, asking in broken
English for work so he could eat.

They gave him raven's bread
and holy water blessed by the abbot

and claimed him as a son
spirited to them for the journey.

His room touched the threshold
of her chapel where candles sang

and ancient voices entered
through the flames, tongues

he had never heard in El Salvador
except once on the radio

when Archbishop Romero called
for the brotherhood of souls.

He notched into his heart
all his growing marks in their love;

they gave him wings, trimmed
from a budget so lean they almost

vanished from self-denial;
but they prospered him as a son,

readying him for the work of prayer
in a world of spiritual poverty.

They never left him;
he hugged them in chaplets,

and on street corners
he heard their unbodied voices pleading

for the breadless, those lost
in time's rocky abyss.

At Mass, he felt them vowing again
he was their child of the promise

as precious as their own blood,
his veins flowing with their kindness.

St. Benedict's Homily on the Temptations of the Flesh

Beloved, beware
the sorcery of the loins
a snake's invitation to taste and see
a patriarch's son stripped; an Egyptian adulteress;
a sleeping father raped; daughters conceiving
despoiling heirs; a Nazorite beguiled
into a kingdom of shorn darkness;
Jezebel's dog-eaten flesh, dung on the fields
deep pits, narrow wells, painted eyes
behind a harlot's veil—
abductions in open country
judgment cloths spread
before elders, women stoned
shrine prostitutes; open temple gates
favors for fertility idols; wilting rocks
a dance of veils; a prophet's head
tetrarchs, scarlet beasts, jeweled cups spilled
offal sheets for Hinnon's fire—
all burning for lust.

Oblates

They serve in monasteries
without walls or cloistered walkways,
the comforts of bells or vows,
the caress of cowls and veils.

They are sent holy into the world.
Their Cluny or Monte Cassino
a borough, a bakery, a bus;
they bring the kindness of God made flesh

to homes, offices, hospitals,
prisons, malls, schools, factories,
banks, courts, the road.

Creation is the kingdom unfurled
on earth where they give God the glory
for leafy boughs and rippled seas,
baptizing rain, fields swelling with fruit,
skies blushing at dawn, bronzed at sunset.

They trace circles on Celtic crosses
asking eternity to ease humanity's sorrow;
and ransom the poor from scrapless pits;
they wear hearts overflowing

with love for gentle community
and carry God's words
in their mouths, a treasury, a pardon,
a breath.

In the *Liturgy of the Hours*
they hear him call their names,
and whisper his.

The Angels

She knew the names of angels
and could hear the sound of their wings, far off

as they flew over her house
sending down signs.

This was her "Manna on 33rd Street,"
feasting those she loved.

Sometimes they left silky feathers,
the quills God uses to write prophecies.

At other times trifoliate leaves,
heaven's calling cards,

or slices of rainbows on rooftops,
shafts of sunrises and sunsets,

slendered light from the ineffable.
The angels had memorized her address.

Holy Communion Is

infinity's gift to time
the hasty bread of Egypt
doves carrying meat to a prophet

the showbread anointed priests feast on
in the sacred silence of the ark

and the corn sweaty apostles pluck
from hot Sabbath fields golden with grain

the Paschal lamb's shank,
smoke climbing to heaven

bags of balm, honey, resin, and almonds
meals for a holy pilgrimage

barley loaves and a few fish
the banquet of belief on a mountain top

the bread of angels
consumed by the faithful

which in turn consumes them

Benedict's Cellarer

St. Benedict would have been proud of her,
the way she managed her household.
A prodigal of smiles, she wasted nothing
but bestowed her bounty on others.
She was rich in God's wealth.

What she received, she pressed down
to give more; her house ran over
with holy measure—pots, pans,
skillets—sacred vessels pouring out
the plenty of hospitality.

She harvested three freezers on her back porch
for the poor, the homeless, gleaners
whose only daily bread came from
what they salvaged from dumpsters.

Her checkbook was full of kept promises.
She rendered unto Caesar what Caesar
failed to render to the least of those
who knocked at her door with bones
fading through their limbs.

Every guest was Christ welcomed
at her table. From the folds of her bosom
came miracles ample as those performed
in the merchant city of Capernaum
or the affluent suburb of Bethany.

Baking for the Carmelites on Dauphin Street

For thirty years or more at Christmas
she baked golden pound cakes
for the cloistered Carmelites
on Dauphin Street in Mobile.

She made each cake look like
Moses's basket in the bulrushes
and placed them before
the iron-barred grate
behind which sin disappeared.

The sisters whose legacy was prayer
smiled at her in sacred silence,
but their eyes promised
heavenly rewards, a hundredfold.

These brides of Christ also baked—
altar bread that transformed tongues
into God's throne.

They prayed for her (when they
were hidden in Christ before God)
in front of the monstrance or in their cells.

In each cake she placed a Christmas wish:
if God ever asked her to be a widow
she would come to Mobile at once
and get engaged to Christ.

The Backdoor to Prophecy

Every Wednesday night she opened
her kitchen backdoor to prophecy—
seven women with lips balmed
with holy unction arrived

and sat in shiny brown folding chairs
in a circle in Mr. Al's den,
invoking the Holy Spirit
so powerfully they stirred him
from his brooding to step
among them, quivering their words.

Then eternity seeped into the room.
For more than two hours, the women glowed
in those thin places between flesh
and spirit, surrendering their tongues
to sounds and syllables unheard in millennia.

She kept a diary of voices,
times, and translations of words that
Ezekiel proclaimed on mountain tops
and Noah caulked into the ark.
Her soul recorded the lexicon of the Essenes.

Dead Sea waves of ecstasy flowed through
these saintly women as their souls
drifted and floated until

they entered God's private catacomb,
beyond the precinct of sleep's power,
to watch the future flow silently before them.

The women often traveled beyond Bethany.

The Prayer Lady's Coffee

She made it strong
enough to withstand tears.

Nothing watered down,
the stark dogma

of a caffeine exorcism,
a jolt for my soul,

current sizzling through my body
making my tongue squirm,

confessing jittery sins,
fidgeting with convenient prayers

I hoped would save me.
You must change your life's

direction, she insisted, pouring more
in my cup, emptying my pretenses

in her kitchen; sip by
sip, the coffee washed away

any excuses, forgetfulness, self-pity,
no easy angels here to protect me.

She had me drink these liquid ashes
to get through this dark night of my soul.

A Family of Souls

In late winter she had a vision
of souls in that third place;
long lines wending up

winding staircases
smothered in fog
pierced every few seconds
by dim shafts of graveyard lights,
their interior fires.

They processed in gabardine tunics
with hoods pulled down over
their moans and abrading tears
on this grim-throated windscape.

But their footfalls did not promise ascent;
they felt only swelling distance.

They carried no shadows to hide
their past in; time died when they did.
They were too burdened with selves
that should have been given away.
How could ashes weigh so much?

She sensed they were her ancestors,
centuries removed from the earth
their corpses turned into;
after four or more generations,

families dissolve into names
without memory.

She prayed for an early Mercy Sunday.

The Garden

Her garden lay between Eden
and the Dead Sea, the city's drainage

ditch running alongside her house
and the chapel garden in the back

with its cascading St. Francis fountain—
water for thirsty, trilling birds.

She spent the summer trimming
and planting rows of daylilies

along the city's clutter, beauty twinned with mortality.
She worked, all 87 pounds, wearing

her wide-brimmed hat, her tallow face streaked
with sweat and dust. How many brown spots

will she wear to the doctor's next month?
But for now she goes on pruning and raking.

As she gardens, she prays about grace
and the necessity of trust, a sparrow

lands on the fountain, sips,
then flies away. *"There's a bit of Scripture*

for today," she smiles. As darkness descends,
she entombs the dead leaves in black plastic bags

and drags them to the street. On the way back,
her face shines lustrous as pearls.

St. Hildegard's Herbs

On the wheel of this great earth
she returned nature
back to where nature first turned
celebrating creation's green glow
planting herbs and noble flowers
below the sinewy loam of her Rhineland:

flowering tansy for catarrh
barley and betony for colicky bouts
dill and fennel to season balms
strong willed garlic and onion
tinctures to heal wounds—
remedies for maladies as old
as the poisonous tribulations
sin infected on the delights of the flesh.

In these seeds of ancient time
she saw visions of angels spinning
in ecstasy before the throne of God
and stars spelling sacred messages
about a second garden not of this world.

In the Month of Blue Moons

She wore two wedding rings
on her one finger
one on top
of the other,
his orbiting hers,
a buckler to fend off
loss.

In the nursing home
he slept
in the hidden half
of his room,
so far away.

His memory eclipsed
traveling
to the dark side
of the moon.

And a penumbra encircled
the place where
his wedding ring
once shone.

Wearing it, though,
she could still feel
the pull of his pulse
in this month of blue moons.

Longing

Our souls are crying, longing
to go home, our legacy

on earth a painful pilgrimage—
seeds sunk in frozen soil,

winter's crop of stark white.
Emmanuel, we hear you

calling in the night, stars
aglow in calm wonder—

the infinity of space that ends
in your embrace beyond death.

Make us plumed birds,
feathers like fingers strumming

a holy lyre, a Psalm
inside a Psalm.

Let our words be wings,
an expanse of ecstasy fleeing

the body's fortress,
the gates of time.

Afterlife

This late-February morning comes
with a wooing sun to waken
azaleas and Sweet William,
but all her dreams have been
postponed until mummy winter passes.

Wrapped tight in frost and forgetfulness,
the icy narcotics of age lock her behind
nameless doors and buzzer voices.

Perhaps when her memory
brightens again and flowers escape
their captivity in stark stalks
embalmed in this void of tears

a new world will arrive
with quilted leaves and butterflies
splashing sprays of color.

Then at last she can pat rouge on,
honeycomb her lips,
and promise the man she loves
an afterlife.

A Hospice Crucifixion

A dirge of cool air flies across
the room as her bed lowers
into an open tomb. Lazarus
sits in a chair nearby
waiting for sundown.
It is the ninth hour.

They swab her mouth with a damp sponge
but she refuses the myrrh,
denying her body what her soul had accepted—
a dry death.

Her veins erupt into welts
from IVs that have scourged
her arms, legs, chest, and stomach.
She wears a purple cloak.

They suction her to listen
for her last words, but her tongue
speaks in yellow gulps and gurgles.
It is finished.

A nurse records her vanishing
vitals. All the sentinels have left.
Who will count her bones?

The bed is stripped
and her tortured shadow
zippered into a body bag.
The hospital insists the mortuary
use the back elevator.

Her family weeps spiced tears
as they line her coffin with linen sheets.

She dreams her wedding veil.
has been torn in two.

The ancient gates open
and martyrs receive her rejoicing,
leading her to the Holy City.

A Holy Woman's Obituary

Her heart lived in monasteries
and rejoiced with the angels over
the fullness of heaven

come to us in this life,
from sunrise to moonset,
the banquet of evermore.

She worked in her yard
amid the turmoil of weeds,
recreating a fulsome Eden.

Her house was a bakery for souls
seeking rest from restlessness,
lives fleeing the flurry and fault of self.

She baked bread for the homeless
and fed a table full of envelopes
begging for her rich mites.

Guardian Dogs

St. Roch or Don Bosco did not love dogs
as much as you did; angels without wings,

they nestled next to you. Fierce prophets
let loose from caves to warn you about

the malice and snares of anyone
who rang your doorbell, unlatched

a door, dared to enter, if only to hug you.
They would have rushed the gates

of hell to pursue your enemies,
chasing them with fury deeper

and deeper into Sheol's pit. They leapt
straight out of *Revelation*.

No wonder their names began
with End Time letters—*Xena, Yowl, Zap.*

Their eyes blazed like meteors
and their hair stood spike stiff.

But you heard Gregorian chants
when they growled, and choirs in their barks.

Father Benedict depended on the raven
for bread; but your dogs would have carried

a pyx around their necks to bring God
home from church for you.

You garlanded them with saints' medals
and blessed each with holy water,

praying for their safety, though
at the end, they lifted you up

for peaceful sleep. After your funeral,
they vanished.

A Nurse Called Joseph

His mother helped
open wombs

and close wounds;
she injected comfort

everywhere in the hospital;
her smile was a hug.

He became a nurse, too,
in places where death spends the night—

nursing homes, hospices,
prison cells. No one ever died

before his shift or after it ended.
Each patient waited

for his touch to carry them
where memory finally lets go of pain.

In his arms they died, their limp limbs
draped over his muscle-chiseled chest

and rock-hewn shoulders, his words
wrapping them softly in sleep.

The Photograph

Before entering the convent she hid
the photo of herself at 21 with long Veronica Lake hair
and hazel green eyes that made men fall
in love with her. She had many offers
from New York and Hollywood.

But God had other productions for her,
those he wrote and directed with a flair for the infinite.
Her eyes became his camera; through them
he presented visions beyond Hollywood's
reeling fabrications.

Dazzling as the Galilee at dawn, her eyes
immersed the souls she prayed over
in twin pools of Bethesda hope and healing,
comfort for those who lived in moans.

When God turned to prophecy, though,
unfolding holy scripts about faraway events,
a deep sleep fell upon her and her face glowed
like St. Bernadette's or the Little Flower's,
two of God's perpetually beautiful stars.

But though she forgot his prophetic words
as soon as she uttered them,
her beauty never left; in her 80s she still looked radiant
as if God used the same makeup on her
he did on the Cherubim and Thrones;
her coiffeur looked like a woven halo.

When packing her things to give to the poor,
her son found the photo she had secreted away
in her closet seven decades ago.

It was her reliquary.

Mr. Al Goes Fishing

Now that she's gone
Mr. Al fishes almost every day
on the lake in his room
on the seventh floor of the hospital,
under a fluorescent sun.

His new john boat is smaller
than the one he left at home;
only the sides are aluminum
and it's not very flat;
sometimes it rocks back
and forth, nearly hurling him
into a pool of red and yellow currents.

His lines, lures, and hooks
hang above his head
so he can slacken or tighten them.
But he wonders how so many hooks could
dig themselves into his arms and legs?

The tackle the hospital supplies
is wobbly, thick, and green,
not thin or easy to cast.
He keeps getting tangled in it
and threatens to complain to the hospital's
fish and game commission.

He misses the peace and quiet
when he fished back home.
The poachers in the lake upstairs
make the fish scream like sirens every night.

During an autumn haze
he catches a glimpse of Jesus walking
on the water and he waves to him

and Jesus waves back and points
toward the very spot Mr. Al
just passed.

Star-speckled bass and rainbow trout,
wearing crowns and archangel wings,
have waited for him a long time.

Parade Ready

Mr. Al went home today
from the veterans' hospital.
He said his goodbyes
to the nurses with golden pins,
but his lips did not move
and his hand could not salute.

His tears felt like ice cubes
as he went out the back
door into a midnight blue Humvee
with granite curtains and
flares blaring along the sides.

He watched the roads
he traveled for years
go by like electricity
through clouds,
but where were all the street signs?

When he arrived,
the carpenter's mate measured him
for a new mahogany uniform
he slipped smartly into,
polished, creased, and crisp
unlike his last faded one
stained red and gory yellow
from all that braid they tied too tight
around his arms and legs.

Then, after he heard
a volley go off
and saw that all the foxholes
were fully manned,
he was parade ready.

The House on 33rd Street

Her children sold her house
as is. Gone are the angels threading
their beads in the corners

of her prayer room, and the candles
smoking now that once flared light,
eternity's perfume trailing behind.

Gone, too, her holy books that blessed
the walls over so many years, packed,
and on their way to the abbey

where the sand-blind abbot
will try to discern the messages
she left in the margins.

The rooms stir in restlessness—
small slips of paper with petitions
waiting to be bedded in her Bible

scatter across the weeping tile floors.
Whenever a window is raised
or a door opens

or closes,
a harmonium of requiems plays—
an orchestra looking
for a conductor.

The green yard she pilgrimaged in
withers and pricks.
Pocked brown splotches

break out everywhere.
Slugs evict the butterflies.

A Manual for Oblates

Her body sleeps in death,
her ashes urned
where spirits breathe softly.

She bequeathed me her *Manual for Oblates*
of St. Benedict, her name and
date written in a wispy hand
beside the name of the monk
who sent it to her seventy years ago.

Now I have been called to scatter
my prayers across its pages.

I have learned that prayers
are not meant to be read
as much as to be inhaled,
each opening, each page
a thurifer, like the cigarette incense
she used to reverence this *Holy Rule*.

This is her relic and my investiture,
this smoke my Black Scapular,
signing me as an Oblate.

The prayers I shall say
nunc et usque saeculum
abound with her breath
still vested in these pages.

What a miracle that her flesh
should course through these
sacred words as I repeat them now.

The Monks at St. Bernard's Cemetery

From their white cypress cells
the monks at St. Bernard's
still obey the rule of work and prayer—
their vows do not stop in death

but continue in wooden chantries,
singing vespers and compline
echoing the voices of their brothers
gathered in cowled rows in the dark church.

From their earthen chapels
they delight in pruning and planting—
blessing oaks, maples, and willows as they reach
for the sun while other monks

tend to the holiness of stones
prayed over in the *Ave Maria Grotto*
with its cleansing waters
washing away soiled time.

Their voices can be heard
on both sides of the cross,
the two worlds of every prayer.

www.ingramcontent.com/pod-product-compliance
Lightning Source LLC
LaVergne TN
LVHW051708080426
835511LV00017B/2793